The Room with Five Walls

The Room with Five Walls

THE TRIALS OF VICTOR HOFFMAN

A Poetic Drama in Two Acts
BY BYRNA BARCLAY

 Prairie Play Series: 24/Series Editor: Diane Bessai

Canadian Cataloguing in Publication Data
Barclay, Byrna
The room with five walls : the trials of Victor Hoffman : a poetic drama in two acts / Byrna Barclay

(Prairie play series ; 24)
ISBN 1-896300-78-2 (pbk.)

1. Hoffman, Victor Ernest, 1946—Drama. 2. Schizophrenia—Drama. 3. Mass murder—Saskatchewan—Shell Lake—Drama.
I. Title. II. Series.

PS8553.A7618R66 2004   C812'.54   C2004-900766-1

Cover photo: Courtesy of The North Battleford News Optimist

NeWest Press acknowledges the support of the Canada Council for the Arts, The Alberta Foundation for the Arts and the Edmonton Arts Council for our publishing program. We also acknowledge the financial support of the Government of Canada through the Book Publishing Industry Development Program (BPIDP) for our publishing activities.

NeWest Press
201-8540-109 Street
Edmonton, Alberta
T6G 1E6
T: (780) 432-9427
F: (780) 433-3179
www.newestpress.com

1 2 3 4 5 08 07 06 05 04

PRINTED AND BOUND IN CANADA ON ANCIENT FOREST-FRIENDLY PAPER

To Mr. Justice George Edward Noble
and Dr. David Keegan, with gratitude

and

The actors in my family; Julianna and Ashley, with admiration

and

Always Ron and Bruce

Contents

Introduction
by Sharon Pollock

Canada's first mass murder was announced in the headlines of
the *Saskatoon Star Phoenix* on 16 August 1967:

> Girl Lone Survivor of Mass Slaying in Shell Lake
> Nine in Farm Family Slain

Five days later the *Phoenix* flashed the good news:

> Leask Man Charged in Mass Murder

As was their legendary wont, the RCMP had got their man. Loner
Victor Ernest Hoffman, age nineteen, was arrested at his family's
farm without a struggle. Reporter Don Harvey described the
young man as "not a bit scared and behaving normally," which
only goes to show that appearances can deceive.

Recently released from a Saskatchewan asylum, Hoffman
had set out to hunt for squirrels in the early hours of 15 August.
Sixty miles from home his Pontiac skidded to a random stop
near a small farmhouse. Hoffman left the car carrying his .22
rifle. Shortly thereafter he returned and drove home to begin
his chores for the day. Nine members of the Peterson family,
whom he previously had never met nor even heard of, lay dead
inside the doorway, in the bedrooms, and in the yard of their
family farm.

The Hoffman case went to trial in 1968. It ended in a verdict of not guilty by reason of insanity for which the legal system should be given some credit, although it is difficult to
believe any other verdict possible given the defendant's personal history, state of mind, and actions. Nevertheless, many
were bothered by testimony which seemed to reveal the defendant's awareness of the nature of his acts: for example, stealing
Jim Peterson's wallet from a bureau and concealing it under a

rock, and picking up shell casings to destroy evidence.

The case resonated in western Canada in ways similar to the reverberation in California of the Manson murders the following year (August 1969). Neither Victor Hoffman's chronic schizophrenia in Saskatchewan nor Charlie Manson's charisma and drugs in Los Angeles met the public's desire and need for clear motivation, coherence and closure. Though distanced geographically, culturally, and circumstantially, both Manson and Hoffman launched changes to perceptions of personal safety and secure space.

In *The Room With Five Walls* playwright Byrna Barclay thrusts an audience inside the disordered mind of Victor Hoffman several decades after the Peterson murders. Hoffman, now an inmate in a maximum security institute for the criminally insane, is confined to a dark and dingy room reminiscent of an underground prison vault. His bleak surroundings may or may not depict reality. The play's "fifth wall" is a surreal wormhole accommodating projections, entrances, and exits.

By reliving his crime's prelude and the subsequent trial, Older Victor engages a resisting Young Victor in a daily search for "the right question" that was never asked, and spurs him on to a diurnal battle with his demons. The Trials of Victor Hoffman must continue, a never-ending quest that mirrors in Victor, despite his illness, the public's own desire and need for an unattainable final resolution or revelation.

Schizophrenia, treatable but not curable, is a puzzling and complex condition. Symptoms include (but are not limited to): delusions; auditory and tactile hallucinations; disordered attention and judgement; emotional and intellectual ambivalence, all of which afflicted Hoffman, and which are manifested most clearly in Young Victor.

It appears that Young Victor harbours the disease and suffers accordingly, while Older Victor has transcended it and is attempting to lead Young Victor to wellness.

But the relationship between the two is more complex than

that. Older Victor is not merely a Master of Ceremonies introducing characters, describing backgrounds and events, and urging Young Victor on to a final confrontation with his (or more correctly their) demons.

Schizophrenic ambivalence can express itself in an individual wishing and not wishing the same thing at the same time; in reacting with pleasant and unpleasant feelings to the same thing; in holding the same and the opposite beliefs at the same time; in stating contradictory things in the same sentence. However prevalent or dominant these symptoms, they do not preclude cognitive thinking in other areas.

Older Victor embodies that ambivalence as well as that cognitive thinking. He is an aspect of Victor Hoffman's schizophrenia, and is both at war with Young Victor and at one with Young Victor.

In this inner world shared with Young Victor, Older Victor is not in complete control of who or what comes and goes. He too hears and sees the demon pigs/angels and often (most clearly near the end) dictates their appearance or vocal presence, as he does that of other characters. But occasionally the demons intrude or interrupt on their own, threatening and commanding Young Victor to "kill kill kill kill."

Though seemingly unaffected by the pigs, shadows of these demons creep into Older Victor's dialogue and that of other characters he has conjured up, their words reflecting his conjuring:

the RCMP Inspector issuing a warning to the culprit:

> "Run with your tail between your legs.
> Hide in a barn."

or Older Victor in describing the manhunt:

> "They nose under every acorn."

Images of implied or actual violence often tint his memory and narrative. In describing the prosecutor:

> "He's not a man you'd want to tangle with in a bar.
> When he orders five beer he holds up the hand
> missing three fingers."

The RCMP Janitor, after trying on Hoffman's boots, fears they could:

> "Turn me into a killer. I'm so mad
> I could just shoot somebody."

Older Victor the first day Mounties drop into the farm:

> "In the field, aggressive
> smell of new mown hay.
> . . . the metallic clang
> when disc hits stone
> like a cell door slamming."

All are subtle reminders that the two Victors are one with the same diagnosis. The younger displays more overt and easily discernible symptoms; those of the older are more suppressed, subtextual, and hidden.

The playwright provides a number of clues to the possible origin of their schizophrenia. Victor's was a difficult birth. His mother recalls:

> ". . . the worst thing
> that ever happened to me.
> Not like the other children,
> he didn't fight
> for his first breath."

Young Victor acknowledges a possible genetic link through his mother:

> "She's like me.
> Doesn't talk well
> to other people."

Hallucinations began at age ten, perhaps triggered by the onset of puberty, hormones, and other environmental stress factors: an overly critical father (a role now assumed by the Older Victor); a vicious rape by school bullies leading to sexual ambivalence. Exposure to farm chemicals might even have played a role. All are hinted at. Maybe some of this, maybe some of that. Medical and mental health professionals have no simple answer.

But answers are what Older Victor wants.

At the beginning of the play he denies Young Victor's plea to go home, his reason being:

> "They asked the wrong question
> at my trial."

Throughout the play a series of possible right questions are proposed by Young Victor:

> "Why did it happen to me?"

by Stella Hoffman, Victor's mother:

> "Why wasn't he helped as he should have been?"

by the Chorus mouthing doctors' questions:

> "What what what what?
> When when when when when?
> Why why why why?"

with Older Victor demanding of Young Victor:

> "Why can't you tell the difference between being guilty
> and making excuses and taking responsibility?"

and finally:

> "Why is there a difference between legal insanity
> and being morally insane?"

There are no answers that suffice; the right question may or
may not have been asked. It is enough to drive back the
demons for another day and escape into the blue of the drug
Haldol. Older Victor grants Young Victor's original request and
offers him release and drug induced visions of home:

> "They'll be back.
> We'll fight Them again
> tomorrow and the next day.
> For now, come with me.
>
> Fall into the blue
> of a winter day
> where the sky is so deep
> you can fall right into it.
> At home, the cock crows at first light.
> Time for chores."

Older Victor is content to drift with the Haldol dreaming of

> ". . . comfort in the smell of the hay,
> the dark corner stall.
> watched only by the barn cats."

The watchful eyes of the cats strike an ominous note, for they
evoke images of their death by clubbing, kicking, stomping,

and starving as detailed by Young Victor, as well as Older Victor's earlier words in answer to the question why?

> "Why why why why.
> Cat in the barn. Crouched
> before a moth, ready to spring,
> whiskers twitching, powerful back legs
> tensed. It leaps suddenly
> to a height undreamed
> by the insect caught."

Despite Young Victor's more tenuous grasp of reality, he recognizes that he can never really go home, and he closes the play with that plaintive statement.

Sharon Pollock
February 2004

The Right to Write

The night of the first staged reading of *The Room With Five Walls* at the Saskatchewan Festival of New Plays a director asked me, "What right do you have to tell this story?"

I suppose it began in 1967 after the first mass murder in Canada when fathers sat up all night with shotguns over their knees. My closest friend slept with a butcher knife under her pillow, and I, the mother of two babies, had a sitter stay with me when my husband was out of town. Like everyone else in my province, I was frightened and fascinated by the Shell Lake massacre, but I didn't know I would one day create a poetic drama in exploration of the event (and mental illness) until my own son was diagnosed as a paranoid schizophrenic and I had acquired a deep knowledge of the illness.

The questions that plague me cannot be answered by the professionals: Why did the mental health system so thoroughly fail Victor Hoffman—and later my son? And, more important perhaps, Why is my gentle boy so unlike the man who was driven to kill nine people he didn't even know?

Through the years, Mr. Justice Noble, who was Victor Hoffman's defence counsel, told me a little more of the story. The mother in me was captured when he said, "What I remember most about the trial was the little Polish mother who wore blue stockings." The writer in me was inspired when he told me how Victor Hoffman saw giant black pigs, horned, no genitals. After slaying nine members of the Peterson family, the shock of what he had done chased away his demons, and afraid of getting caught, he counted the empty cartridges on a sewing machine, realizing that some were missing. In search of them, he lifted a blanket from a bed and between two dead children found four-year-old Phyllis. When Mr. Noble asked why he didn't kill her, Victor answered, "She was only a little girl. I would never hurt a human."

Not knowing what form the narrative would eventually demand, I began writing poetry in search of the central metaphors of the story, finding them first in the taped confession: the hawk, the squirrels, the yellow coyote. When I read that Victor Hoffman, now fifty, has a new pair of binoculars and that the corner room in Ward B has five walls, I found the title and the technique I needed to dissolve time and bring the past into the present. Soon the characters began talking to each other, and the poetic drama emerged in two acts, the first exploring the events that led up to the murders, the second showing an older and stabilized Victor suffering a fate worse than death by hanging, for every day he must live with the memory of the trial and of the murders.

I have no answer for the director. Perhaps I have no right to refuse or turn away from a story that arrived as a gift or from the artistic stretch that poetry and drama demands of a novelist.

Byrna Barclay
February 2004

Production History

The Room With Five Walls: The Trials of Victor Hoffman was featured at the Saskatchewan Playwrights Centre Festival of New Plays in 2002.

C A S T

Old Victor	*Kelly Henderek*
Young Victor	*Jason Fedoruk*
Stella Hoffman	*Michele Sereda*
Robert Hoffman	*Robert Benz*
Chorus and Others	*Cavan Cunningham, Tom O'Hara, Michele Sereda, Robert Benz*

Dramaturges	*Ben Henderson and Stephen Heatley*
Director	*Linda Moore*

The 2004 co-production between Curtain Razors and the University of Regina Theatre Department featured the following:

C A S T

Older Victor	*Tom O'Hara*
Young Victor	*Jayden Pfeifer*
Stella Hoffman	*Michele Sereda*
Robert Hoffman	*TBA*
Chorus and Others	*Katie Bowes, Ken McLeod, Alan Long, Michele Sereda, Maki Yi*

Set Design	*Wesley D. Pearce*
Lighting Design	*Jason Dubois*
Director	*Chris Gerrard-Pinker*

PLAYWRIGHT'S NOTE ABOUT THE TEXT

With each production, the director's artistic choices may vary from the original script according to his/her interpretation of the playwright's vision. Certain adaptations in the above productions varied from the playscript presented here.

Production Note

This two act drama takes place in the Holding Unit of Ward B in Oak Ridge, Division of Penetangeshene Mental Health Centre, the maximum security hospital for the criminally insane in Ontario.

The entire drama unfolds in the inner landscape of Victor Hoffman. A simple setting may involve a corner room, with the mobile fifth wall the entry and exit into the past, particularly the events that led up to the mass murders at Shell Lake, Saskatchewan in August, 1967, and the trial of Victor Hoffman in January, 1968.

Young Victor moves from his cot, stage left (from the audience perspective), to take part in the scenes from the past that occur centre stage. Older Victor remains stage right, controlling the binoculars and the fifth wall. Because Older Victor is selective in what he wants Young Victor to remember, each person from the past may be illuminated by spotlights so the others in the scene, especially in the courtroom, are diminished or not seen at all.

The Chorus are voices inside Young Victor's head, representing his angels and horned demons in the form of giant black pigs, and they do not appear until the scene when he drives them away.

CHARACTERS
Victor Hoffman, age 50
Young Victor, age 19
Robert Hoffman, Victor's father
Stella Hoffman, Victor's mother
George Edward Noble, Defence Counsel
Mr. Justice Murdoch Alexander McPherson Jr.
Members of the RCMP
Various patients and staff of Saskatchewan Hospital, North
    Battleford .
The Townspeople and Jury
The Chorus

NOTE
This drama may be considered an ensemble piece, with a few
actors playing many parts.

ACT I

Scene 1
The Room With Five Walls

Lights slowly rise.
Dark as a dungeon, the corner room
in Ward B has a rusty toilet, corroded
sink, one paper cup, a cot.
Victor Hoffman looks through
a new pair of binoculars at the fifth wall.

Older Victor

I can never go home now.
But if I could, I'd like to see
the man-made lake and Blackstrap mountain
they built after I was put away.
Wouldn't that be something?

I read that the mountain rises from the valley floor
where once Indians chased buffalo
and hunting was always good.

Thirty years have passed
since I went hunting. I followed
the spiralling hawk,
my yellow coyote.

From my corner room at the Ridge
I can only look back. Trying to see
my Saskatchewan home
far beyond Georgian Bay
through a new pair of binoculars.

I've almost got it.
It's coming into focus.

Sound of gears grinding as wall begins to open. Light remains dim centre stage. Mist begins to rise as if from a river.

> Now I see the farm, my home.
> There's my mother.

Spotlight on Stella Hoffman centre stage.

Stella Hoffman
Victor, I can't see no pigs!

> **Older Victor**
> She waves her apron, a surrender flag
> at my father in the field.

Spotlight on Robert Hoffman.

Robert Hoffman
Somethin's wrong
with that boy.
He's a hard worker, good at cleanin'
the barn and loadin' manure onto the stoneboat,
but he don't know his own strength.
He broke the pitchfork handle.

Everything you tell him goes in one ear, twists around,
and comes out t'other backwards
like the crankcase he took apart
and couldn't fit back into the block.
What comes over my boy, what goes on
in that thick head of his? Pulling his red hair out
by the fistful. Why is this happening
to Victor? Where did I go wrong?

> **Older Victor**
> I've got him in my sights.

Young Victor enters, gun in hand.

Young Victor
Stop it!
Not again!

> **Older Victor**
> Watch the yellow coyote skulk
> through the pine and spruce,
> scuttle into its lair.

Young Victor
I was only twelve first time I saw it.
Dad took me hunting, but I couldn't shoot
the coyote. It turned tail, looking over his shoulder
at me not yet a man.

> **Older Victor**
> The hawk hovering
> over the henhouse takes flight
> with an ominous cry.

Red light on fifth wall.

Young Victor
Don't make me do this again.
Let me go home and stay there.

> **Older Victor**
> Never.

Young Victor
Why? What is it
with you and the binoculars?

> **Older Victor**
> They asked the wrong question
> at my trial.

Chorus
Why, why, why, why?

Young Victor
Why did it happen to me?
I didn't choose to go mad.

                                        Older Victor
                    Exactly. But that's not the right question either.

Young Victor
Here they come again! The giant pigs!

On bended knee, Young Victor takes aim.

                                        Older Victor
                            You don't shoot at the yellow coyote,
                                        or the hawk, not even
                                        at tin cans lined up
                                    like crows on the fence.

Sounds of gunshots.

Robert Hoffman
As far as I can see,
my son fires at the chimney or TV antenna,
at his mother cowering behind the wringer washer
on the front stoop, at poplar trees, the tops
of outbuildings.

Victor scatters empty shells on gravel,
like chicken bones
left by his yellow coyote.
He rises, arms raised to the sky.

Young Victor
Why do they appear to me,
like a calling? Rising
from the volcanic bowels of the earth
in a foreign land. They fill me with unholy light.

Older Victor

It's not like receiving grace at the altar,
where I prayed Jesus would not forsake me,
a boy who tried to be good
but could never do anything right
to please the heavenly Father,
or my accusing one on earth.

Young Victor

Jesus drove the demon swine
over the cliff of the sky.
That's what they are, giant pigs,
black as the burnt bush.

Hysterical laughter from Chorus.

Young Victor

For more than forty days and forty nights
They have come to me in this wilderness,
upright on their cloven hooves.

Older Victor

Naked! No genitals!

Young Victor starts shooting again. Sounds of gunshots.

Young Victor

I aim at an eye. *Gunshot sound.*
A throat. *BANG*
Behind a shoulder
where lies the heart. *BANG*
Why do the bullets pass through them?
Sobbing.

Older Victor

Stop them!

Young Victor
They're making war
on angels!

Older Victor
Prove you are a man.
Drive them away!

Young Victor rises, whirls,
firing and missing, molten tears
blurring his eyes.

Young Victor
Bullets spent. But I can't stop shooting.
My shoulder aches
from the kick of the rifle butt.

Older Victor
The swine fold into themselves,
their light drains like foul water
into a ditch. It lifts like a finale
of northern lights.

Red light goes to black.
Robert Hoffman holds Young Victor
by the shoulders.

Robert Hoffman
Son, listen to me!
We're taking you to the hospital.

Stella Hoffman
You'll be safe there, Victor.

Older Victor
The asylum was far from safe.

The Hoffmans lead him away, exit.

Spotlights go to black.
Low sound of coyote howling.

Scene 2
It Isn't a Place You'd Ever Want to Visit

> **Older Victor**
> It was crammed, chock full to the rafters:

Young Victor
With murderers.
Rapists.
Hookers.
Idiots.

> **Older Victor**
> The deaf and the mute.
> It's what they don't say
> that must be remembered.

Young Victor
People who can't stop boozing
    who have forgotten how to laugh
    who never speak
    who cry too much.

Once put away in the mental
you never get out again.

> **Older Victor**
> Windows barred. Doors padlocked. To keep out
> unwanted visitors.

Young Victor
Just seeing it from the gravel road
gives me the shivers.

Older Victor
Here, rain is God weeping for the living.

Young Victor
In the garden: robotic men and women
bend over hoes, spades.
Get close enough and you'll die
of fright.

This is the mad house!

Older Victor
Screams don't stop.
Lights never turned off.

Young Victor
It's enough to make you crazy.

Older Victor
I vomited on the stairs.

Stella Hoffman
Don't worry, son. This is a safe place.

Robert Hoffman
They can make you
stop laughin'
when nothin' is funny.

Chorus
Don't think we won't find you, you, you.
We are everywhere, where, where.

Young Victor
Don't leave me here!

Robert Hoffman
It's likely only for a week.
I need you on the farm.

Stella Hoffman
Maybe you can work in the garden.

Robert Hoffman
Mother and I will visit.

Young Victor
After my folks leave
they take away my clothes.
I can't run away in pyjamas.

First Aide
When it's decided where you'll work
you'll get institution pants, shirt, shoes.

> **Older Victor**
> Between two bull-headed men
> who could wrestle Herefords
> you are taken to your ward.

Second Aide
A husky guy like you could operate
the heavy machine that cleans floors.

First Aide
The top floor is the halfway ward.
Just be glad you ain't startin'
in the basement. No beds. No bathrooms.
Just the sleepless. Climbin' walls.

Young Victor
How many people in here?

Second Aide
In its heyday, two thousand,
now the government's downsizing
maybe nine hundred. Men
separated from women.

First Aide
So don't get any fancy ideas.
Them's peepholes for staff.

Young Victor
Ceilings so high. I feel like a bug.
White globes above, many shining planets.

> **Older Victor**
> Walls so thick a choir of angels
> could sing hosannas
> and never be heard in this hall.

Young Victor
The cells look like horse stalls.

Second Aide
These are holding units
for people who want to hurt themselves,
who can't behave.

> **Older Victor**
> Another heavy door
> with black lettering:
> THE TREATMENT ROOM.

Young Victor
Everyone wears white.
The woman mopping the floor.
The nurse carrying a tray of pills in tiny paper cups.
They could be angels in disguise.

Older Victor
You see into a ward.

Young Victor
Bigger than the gymnasium at school.
The walls orange as vomit. Smell
of old.

Older Victor
Shroud-wrapped men in geri-chairs,
mouths agape, tongues lolling.
Staff lined up against the walls
watch them snore, drool, moan.

Young Victor
Maybe a hundred of them.

First Aide
That ward is for people born here.

Young Victor
One guy as tall as Jesus
with winter-blue eyes
paces. Hands in his pants. Jerking off.

Chorus
A sin before god and man.

Older Victor
I wanted to see a pied piper
leading the old children
with wreaths in their hair,
bearing bright balls,
bubble-pipes, balloons.

Chorus
Suffer the little childen.

Young Victor
I escape into my ward.
It's rooster-shit yellow.

A guy in garden-green pants, purple suspenders,
flies into the cavernous room, whirls,
puts a fist through the door.

The Prophet
The world is ending!

> **Older Victor**
> He became my only friend,
> The Prophet, who worked
> beside me in the laundry,
> emptying foul clothesbags
> into vats of boiling water.

The Prophet
I just know, that's all. One day
you will kill someone.

> **Chorus**
> Off to prison you must go,
> you must go, you must go.
> Off to prison you must go,
> my fair farmboy, oh.

The Trials of Victor Hoffman

Scene 3
Mind Alterations

Older Victor
At night, a hundred cots so close
I smelled Haldol-breaths,
the stench metallic,
like soldered metal.

At first light, outside the treatment room,
the chosen do the Haldol shuffle down the hall.
Some wheeled from their wards on stretchers.
Rumble of rubber tires on hardwood.
Others strapped into ancient chairs.
Grumble and creak of old wicker.
Whir of newer, padded perambulators.

Young Victor
In front of me: a woman with no teeth.

Older Victor
She combs her long cobweb hair.

Woman with White Hair
I likes being zapped so much
even when I'm on the outside
I asks my doctor to shock me
whenever I feels the need
to forget the unspeakable.

Young Victor
One by one, names are called,
by the male nurse the patients call St. Peter.
Each one is taken into the room.

Chorus
An Angel: Not me! I'll be good.
A Devil: I rebuke you!

Old Victor
Some whimpering. Others crying.
One by one, they're carried out
on stretchers, wheeled back to their wards,
spittle leaking from their lips.

The Prophet
It's like jump-starting your car.
It keeps the nurses running.

Young Victor
The prophet's on a new drug,
his Jesus eyes bluer
than the halo of the Holy Ghost.

The Prophet pivots
in the doorway, raises his arms
as if nailed to the cross.

The Prophet
Father, forgive them!

Aides yank The Prophet
backwards into the room.
The heavy door slams shut.

Young Victor
I feel like an eye-witness
to the atomic bomb.

Older Victor
I tried to run for the exit
at the end of the hall.

Aides enter with gurney,
wrestle Young Victor onto it,
strap his legs and arms.

Older Victor

Then it all happens so fast:
the light above a Nimbus.
A disembodied hand
shoves the bit between my teeth.
A forked river of light
explodes inside my head,
my mind goes bang.

Sound of gunshot.

just as it did the morning
of the murders.
I leave my jerking body.
Float with angels on high.

Chorus

You'll be safe, safe, safe,
with us, us, us.

Older Victor

A nurse wipes drool from my chin.
The doctor watches the needle
on the machine: a metronome.
They're part of a cult, with their look-in-the-eyes
and shine-the-penlight, waggle-your-finger
and turn the dial to off.

Young Victor

High above me
my body
        hangs by the neck
with an electrical cord   sizzling
        from the last white-hot globe.

Older Victor
I smelled singed fur.
Eyes of the yellow coyote
rolled back,
only the whites showing.

The body slumps,
one last spasm, a chasm opens
for my re-entry. Into the white world.
Where the doctors
asked all the wrong questions.

Chorus
What, what, what, what?
When, when, when, when, when?
Why, why, why, why?

Aides help Young Victor off gurney, then exit.
Young Victor staggers around, centre stage.

Older Victor
For days, under the white-hot globes
I groped down long halls, through
a tunnel into the games room,
unable to turn a dial on the radio,
its static like lost bees
calling home to the hive.
I couldn't name the TV antenna,
the screen a snowfall of forgotten words.

I couldn't remember my driver's licence,
how many times I failed grade nine.

Young Victor
I'm afraid
to plug in the heavy machine
and clean the floors,
of a match struck

in the smoking room,
of Haldol, the drug
that feels like electric charges
zapping up and down my spine.

The shocks—

Older Victor
Twelve of them!

Young Victor
—didn't chase away
the devil-swine.

    Chorus
    Kill, kill, kill
    something big,
    bigger than a hawk,
    hawk, hawk, hawk,
    bigger much bigger
    than a squirrel, squirrel,
    bigger much bigger than a coyote,
    coyote, coyote, coyote.
    big big, big as a pig.

Scene 4
What Ever Happened to Victor?

Older Victor
Shock. Rape. Memory. Loss.
But it comes back. In therapy
I remembered Denise.

No one in my family ever talked
about what happened in the boys' bathroom.

Stella Hoffman
The less said about it the better.

Robert Hoffman
Best forgotten.

Young Victor
It could have been '63, the year
Dad bought the maroon Pontiac
but wouldn't let me drive it
till I got my learners.

> **Older Victor**
> Have you no shame?

Young Victor
It has nothin' to do with me.

> **Older Victor**
> Who are you?

Young Victor
I'm half man, half woman!
Denise is female.

> **Older Victor**
> She took over my brain
> so long ago I'm not sure
> if it was before or after
> the principal wanted charges laid.

Young Victor
It would have made it all worse for Denise
if I squealed on the bully, the guys in his gang.
Somehow they knew she was inside me.
They went after Denise. Not me!

Older Victor
Denise wasn't real!
Face it. What happened in the bathroom?

Young Victor *Pacing.*
Boys at urinals,
bully moving in, his gang.
The kick and punch.
Flailing my arms,
knocked onto my back.
Too many holding me down. Kicking.
Jeans torn off, shirt.
The flip onto my belly.
Bloody nose.
Hard to breathe.
Horselaughs. Me cursing them.
Legs spread, the pain.

Older Victor
You saw beneath cold tile
a field in summer fallow.

Young Victor
Waves of water,
the Red Sea dividing,
columns falling on Denise.
The earth opened.
Demon-pigs rose up.

Hysterical laughter from Chorus.

I can't even say what entered me.
It couldn't happen to me, so strong
I can bend a crow bar, horseshoes.
I want to run away
from the town, school, the farm, my Dad.

Older Victor
Alone, you were always alone after that.

Young Victor
Where can I go?

Young Victor runs to cot stage left, fusses with blankets.

In the '63 Pontiac I made a bed to die in.
Gunnysacks over the garage windows.
Rags in the exhaust pipe. Voices
inside the disconnected radio.

> **Chorus**
> We need you, you, you.
> Come with us, us, us.

Young Victor lies down on cot.

Young Victor
The trouble with angels:
they can hear you
thinking.

> **Chorus**
> **One Angel:** Just go to sleep, sleep, sleep.

Young Victor
My head on a pillow stuffed with chicken feathers.
Scratchy. Throat raw. Smell of gas.
Tastes like machine oil. Windows steamy.

> > **Older Victor**
> > In the clearing: a silver sword.
> > An angel's wing, like a palm
> > slapped the side window. A disembodied voice:

Stella Hoffman *Offstage.*
Victor! Victor!

Older Victor

Door yanked open.
You fell out, into the blue. Blue.
The sky was as blue as Mother's stockings.
As her breathing
into your mouth.

Young Victor

For days I locked an animal
in the garage, starved it.
I'm no better than the cat I found
caught in a magpie trap.

Scene 5
After Angels

Older Victor

The first time you saw angels
magpies circled you
alone in the field
forced to burn roots
with matches
you carried in a glass jar.

Young Victor

After Sunday School hellfire
I'm afraid to light the cookstove.
Even the oil heater might explode
if I don't watch it.

Older Victor

Wanting to fly a toy plane
over the timberline,
you soldered a metal stem
to a bigger gas tank,
pumped in air.

Young Victor
Into a snow bank
the explosion sent me flying.

> **Older Victor**
> Where no birds nested
> you found feathers.

Young Victor
The devils killed the angels!

Scene 6
Letters from the Asylum: First Calling Home

Young Victor
What are you doing now?

> **Older Victor**
> Reading the letters
> you wrote in the asylum.
> They may be important
> to the question. See for yourself.
> .

Young Victor
July 12, 1967.
Mum and Dad, hello.
I had a talk with my doctor. I can go home
in two weeks time, that's on the 23rd of July.

I feel different about life now,
wish I had got my grade nine.
Never ever taught this way before.

> **Older Victor**
> Watch your spelling.

Thought. Not taught.
Skip to the last letter.

Young Victor
Doesn't it hurt you to remember?

Older Victor
It's got to be done.

Young Victor
July 20, 1967.
I did get to see my doctor
but he did not say much;
he was so very busy. All he said was:
"We shall see when the day comes."

He'll have a long talk with you.

It's just awful here.
I'm working in the laundry,
hard work, and hot.
I'm sorry my writing is small.
I'm trying to write bigger.

Don't leave me here, please don't
leave me here.

Robert Hoffman
Victor was there until July 26th.
When we picked him up
I could see he was still sick.
The doctor was having lunch, wouldn't see us.
No one told us the importance of him takin' his pills,
or about the clinic in Prince Albert.

No! Never a history of mental illness
in my family!

Older Victor
There is now!

Stella Hoffman
What could we do?
We would have done anything they asked us,
but they never talked to us
about Victor's illness.

Older Victor
Well, do you get it now?

Young Victor
Just the doctor part.
I never get nothin' but trouble
with demon-pigs, them voices
that won't ever quit.

Hysterical laughter from Chorus.

Older Victor
I want you to let them go!

Young Victor
Go where?

Scene 7
Cover Up

Wall opens. Spotlight on Chief of Staff.

Young Victor
I don't ever want to see that guy again!

Older Victor
Why not?

Young Victor
He shocked me. Twelve times!

Older Victor
I hope you find what he says
about you and Mum and Dad
important to the question.

Chief of Staff
How could I explain to simple-minded people
the nature of Victor's illness,
that he saw the devil, that he would have to stay
in the asylum for more than a year?
The Hoffmans wanted to take him home.
I don't believe they made three trips
before they even met me.

When they did take him home, two months later,
the receptionist didn't tell them
I was too busy to see them!
The head nurse gave them pills to last a month.
They should have known how important it was
for Victor to take the medication. To hide
the guns.

Robert Hoffman said Victor was heavily drugged, stiff,
and it took three days before he started to come out of it.
It was a reaction to being released.
He didn't want to take the pills.

Once someone is released, my job is finished.
Victor signed himself in,
and he signed himself out.

Scene 8
Driven

Older Victor
When I got home from the hospital
I couldn't sleep. That swelling again,
in the right side of my head,
I was driven by the Voices:

Chorus
Kill. Kill something big.

Young Victor
I abandon the crankshaft,
fill the tank of my grey Plymouth
with gas from the barrel by the bush.
Roar out of the yard, down the road
to the new blacktop highway
up to Kilwinning, straight north,
past the turnoff to Shell Lake,
west along Highway 3.
I want to see how thick the spruce
where squirrels ready for winter
promise good hunting.

Chorus
No, not big enough.

Near the school house
a nighthawk looking for woodmites
lifts off, catches
an updraft, loops,
swoops down
onto a telephone pole.

Chorus
Not big enough.

Something goes bang in my head.

Sound of gunshot.

Chorus pants.

The Plymouth skids, I slam
on the brakes, shoot past a farm.

Chorus
Not that one!

Stop beyond the lane. There
to my left another farm, white
house, green trim peeling.

Older Victor
The August moon yields
to a strong break of day.

Young Victor
Along the ditch lopes
the yellow coyote.

Chorus
No! Still not big enough!

Young Victor
I open the gate,
drive into the farmyard,
leave the Plymouth,
the preying hawk,
the skulking yellow coyote.

Carefully close the gate.

Enter a house.
.22 rifle in hand.

> **Older Victor**
> Later, when I left
> no one had seen me
> or what I did.
> Even the waiting coyote
> lost its voice.

Young Victor
Can't you stop now?

> **Older Victor**
> I want you to see the funeral.

Young Victor
You're meaner than Dad!

Scene 9
In God's Green Acres

Behind wall: shadows of crowd, graves.
Sound of a crowd in hushed tones.

> **Older Victor**
> You never saw so many folks in your life.
> Too many to count in God's Green Acres.
> Not even the legion hall could hold them,
> never a church. I'd say
> a couple of thousand from God-knows-where.

Young Victor
The guards said some people
saw me at the funeral.
I don't know how I could be

in two places at the same time.

Older Victor
The graveyard is awash in colour
as if the sky opened
and God dropped petals.
It's because of the women,
their flowery dresses, hats big as geraniums,
Jackie Kennedy pillboxes.

A police photographer snaps the crowd
come to pay last respects to the Petersons.
Inspector Sawyer's men take down
licence plate numbers
just in case one belongs to the killer.

This is the Mounties' first mass murder,
hell, the first in all of Canada.

The service is supposed to last
only seventeen minutes
so the Mounties can get back
to their manhunt. A whole posse
guarding Phyllis at some neighbour's.

Here comes the procession.
Led by Anglican priests:
Reverend Gerald Spence of Leask,
Canon Douglas Gregory from Meadow Lake.
They part the crowd
like Moses did the Red Sea.

There's the Guard of Honour
from the Royal Canadian Legion,
every one with eyes red-rimmed, blood-
shot. Hungover as hell, I bet. Just because
Lance Corporal Jim Peterson
in World War II took a bullet

in his shaving kit instead of his heart.
It's not funny like it was when he told it
in the beer parlour.

Beneath a solitary spruce, a common grave.
The Canadian flag on Peterson's coffin,
red roses on his wife's. A single sweetheart
on each of the children's.

The baby's body will be buried with his mother.

Young Victor
When I die I want to be buried
with my mother.

Sound of bugle playing taps/Last Post.

Older Victor
No headstones. Only black markers, white lettering:

James, F.H.

I wonder why no dates.

Young Victor
I don't want to hear the names!

Older Victor
Evelyn M. 1925-1967.
Jean M. 1950-1967.
Mary J. 1954 -1967.
Dorothy E. 1956-1967.
Pearl E. 1957-1967.
William J. 1961-1967.
Colin A. 1964-1967.
Larry F. 1966-1967.

Bugle stops.

Spotlight on Anglican Priest.

Anglican Priest
I went to the Peterson home with the police
and identified the family, each one lying
where they had been shot,
but in the midst of all that terror and pain
an unseen hand stretched out,
and a power touched each one.
On each face was a look of calm and peace-
ful quiet.

Young Victor *Weeping.*
I didn't know those people.
You win. What do you want?
I'll do anything
to make you stop!

> **Older Victor**
> You always said that to the devil-pigs.
> And then you obeyed them!

Young Victor
You're one of them!
You're on their side?
I hate you.

> **Older Victor**
> Too bad. We're locked in
> this search.

Scene 10
Manhunt

Spotlight on Inspector Sawyer.

RCMP Inspector
I want the lunatic who wiped out that family
in manacles and leg irons by sundown
or every man on this force turns in
his kit and hangs up his red serge. Understand?
Let me make myself perfectly clear.
Tomorrow you take up ditch digging.
Run with your tail between your legs.
Hide in a barn. Let me tell you
those rednecks aren't sitting up all night
with pitchforks so they're ready for haying.
Or with guns and hunting knives
waiting for geese to fly south.

I want four teams, seventy-five men in each,
spread out in a twenty-mile grid
around the Peterson place. Here! Here! And here!
I want patrol cars, officers and dogs
dispatched from point to point to point,
closing in. There! There! And there!
Search out weapons in every farm house,
shed, granary. Even outhouses.

All owners of .22 caliber rifles
must fire two shots. Spent casings
will be flown immediately
to the crime lab in Regina.

Are you still with me? Listen up!

I want to know if Peterson had enemies,
who held a grudge against him and why.

Find out if any strangers were in town
on the night of August 15th. Search
every garage and station for gas receipts,
then trace all vehicles not registered to locals.

Corporal Nolan
I've got a tip from a farmer
forty-five miles from the scene of the crime.
The suspect is armed.

Inspector
Take five good men with you.

Scene 11
If I Run They'll Shoot Me Down

Young Victor
They're coming after me!

Older Victor
In the field, smell
of new mown hay.
Heavy hum of the tractor.
I'm riding the mower,
watching for unearthed boulders,
the metallic clang
when a disc hits stone
like a cell door slamming.

In the pasture, cows
lumber into the shelter belt.
Twigs snap, crushed by heavy boots.
Scrub brush rioting, branches
breaking, leaves like feathers
fluttering up. The hawk
swoops down

on a bloody hare half-flying
half-hopping on three legs
out of the bush. In hot pursuit
a police dog with a bloody muzzle.

Corporal Nolan
Heel, Rex! Goddammit, heel!

Older Victor
Mounties everywhere.
Thick as a forest, as underbrush, as prairie wool.
Labradors sniff at spoor, coyote tracks.
They nose under every acorn.
Not a pebble unturned. A leaf left.
They're looking for spent cartridges.

Young Victor
They don't have a clue.

Older Victor
Cruisers churn up dust. Gravel flying.
Two patrol cars roar into the yard.
Six Mounties get out.

Young Victor
Dad unloads bales from the hay rack.
The corporal asks Dad:

Corporal Nolan
How many guns have you got?

Robert Hoffman
Just two, I think.

Young Victor
Dad leads them to my grey Plymouth
where he must think I left the .303 rifle
after deer hunting on the other farm.

Instead, he finds lying across the back seat:
the .22 fitted with my homemade firing pin.

Robert Hoffman
We use it to scare off rustlers and bears,
usually leave it hangin' in the garage.

Robert Hoffman removes five bullets for the Mountie.

Older Victor
I threw seventeen spent cartridges
far into the bush.

Young Victor
They won't find the wallets
I took from the bureau
and hid in the crevice
of a rock too big to budge
without a crowbar.

Older Victor
On the front stoop they found
my rubber boots.

Young Victor
Without them
my feet will get wet.

Robert Hoffman
You'll get them back.

Older Victor
That night police cruise
up and down the borders of our farm.

Young Victor
If I run they'll shoot me down,
not even ask questions.

Older Victor
The next morning,
the police return with a warrant.

Sound of police dog barking.

Corporal Nolan
Move in!

Older Victor
The cops tow away my Plymouth.

Young Victor
They seize my blood—
stained jeans,
polka dot handkerchief,
my leather gloves!

The next thing I know
I'm under arrest!

Older Victor
Leaving the yard in the police car
I look back
at Mum and Dad,
at the homeplace
I will never see again.

Young Victor
In the underbrush, I saw
the yellow eyes of the coyote.

Young Victor returns to cot, stage left.

Don't you know
how sorry I am?

Scene 12
Believe me

Young Victor slumps in jail cell, composing a letter to his parents.

Older Victor

Saturday, September 8, 1967.

If only the world could read my letter.

Young Victor
Believe Me i am very sorry for what I have done to myself &
the Peterson family & all the grief that i caused you believe
me i did not know what i was really going to do that morning
when i was working on the engine but i suddenly was unable
to work on it anymore & i recall looking at my watch & it was
five o'clock & then i did not know what to do & i began pacing
until a swelling feeling began to grow on the right side of my
head & then it went down my right side to my toes & it made
me feel light   free   brave   and the desire to kill   even to kill
you & the whole family & i should drive for an hour on
Saturday the day you went to the fair   i took the crankcase &
went outside to wash it with gasoline but the door began to
shake & somebody was working the knob   violently i opened
the door as quick as i could & stepped outside but no one was
there   later as i was putting the engine together i was aware
that somebody was watching me but i just kept working on the
engine.

I hope the kids at school aren't bugging Allen.
Dad, don't work too hard on those bales yourself.
Mum, you should order a pair of Sunday overalls for the trial,
something more decent. There is plenty of money of mine
which you are keeping.

Young Victor returns to cot, stage left.

Young Victor
I meant every word.

Scene 13
His Father's Last Words

Wall opens, spotlights on Robert Hoffman and Young Victor in jail cell, centre stage.

Robert Hoffman
When you was arrested
I never cried
so hard in all my life.
It pretty near killed me.

Did you kill those people?

> **Older Victor**
> On the other side of the bars
> separating me from my father,
> for the first time
> I saw disembodied hands wafting
> nearer and nearer my throat.

Young Victor
I shot the demon-pigs.
I wasn't myself.

> **Older Victor**
> Hogshit, you weren't yourself!
> For once be a man for Dad!
> Be responsible!

Robert Hoffman
How did you get out of the house
without me hearin' you?

Young Victor
You should've chased after me.
Then it wouldn't have happened.

Robert Hoffman
How could you pump so much lead into them?

Young Victor
I didn't know what I was doing.
You can't hate me
more than I hate myself.

Older Victor
Look at the hands!
Going for your throat!
Steel hands,
twisted like iron rope,
strong as a hammer, an axe.

Young Victor
If I had used an axe
I never would have been nabbed.
They had ballistics with the gun.

Robert Hoffman
If you commit a crime you—

Young Victor
—hang!

Robert Hoffman
When you was home
I was proud of you.
Now that son has died
with the Peterson burial.

Maybe it will be easier
on both of us
if I never see you again.

Robert Hoffman shoves his work-worn hand through the bars.
Young Victor weeps.

Scene 14
Prisons

In jail, Victor sheds his shirt,
rips his pants.
Naked. On all fours,
he scrambles forward,
scurries back,
tosses his head.

Older Victor
You're trying to get away from them,
huge black swine on hind legs,
with great opened snouts.

Young Victor snarls.

Young Victor
They swell. Inside
my rib cage. Break
my head against high walls.

Older Victor
They tricked you.
They said squirrels and hawks were too small. Even
your yellow coyote baying at the moon.

Young Victor howls.

Older Victor
What they made you do
was against the laws of man.
Their authority was higher

than my father's. Even Reverend Post's.

Young Victor
Prayers won't save me.

Young Victor squats on his haunches.

I can't see so good no more.
I had a vision.
I'm gettin' terrible weak.

Older Victor
That swelling feeling is growing again
in your head.

Young Victor
Why there should be a death sentence
is because I want to die.

Young Victor weeps until lights out.

ACT II

Scene 1
The Soul of the Courthouse

> **Older Victor** *Pompously.*
> These halls of justice, this sceptered edifice,
> the oldest courthouse in the province
> understands revenge.

Young Victor
I don't ever want to see it again.

> **Older Victor**
> It knows about failure! Fear of the unknown!
> Why the criminal justice system
> is the only one that can never say, "No."
> When the gavel bangs
> it is heard by the comatose.

Chorus
Hush, hush, hush.

Young Victor
I was locked up
in one of the basement cells
where prisoners are held
while awaiting trial.
At night, the courthouse is haunted!

> **Older Victor**
> It smells of musk, old sweat, human wastes.
> Echoes with the clank of spurs on cellar stairs,
> the chinckle of handcuffs
> when wrists are rubbed together.
> Daily, black-robed barristers hustle

                              down a long corridor
                         to the Queen's Bench courtroom
                         where the dias looks like an altar.
                    Underlings lug briefcases, boxed documents,
                              the criminal code of Canada.
                              Only these walls know
                         what was said by sequestered juries.
                              There is always a motif
                              if not motive for murder.

Young Victor
You can't make me remember.

                                        Older Victor
                              Here Victor Ernest Hoffman was tried
                                   in January, 1968.
                              Today, the sky is white,
                    snow falling on hunched shoulders, bowed heads.
                         Townspeople, farmers, media huddle
                         together for warmth, stamping cold feet,
                         breathing into the cups of gloved hands.
                         They have waited for this day since August
                              when fathers sat up all night
                              with shotguns over their knees,
                              and women hid butcher knives
                                   under their pillows.

Young Victor
No one was as afraid as me.

                                        Older Victor
                         After he heard my confession on tape,
                         the prosecutor's assistant went home
                         and slept beside his daughter's crib.

Young Victor
How do you know?

Older Victor
Everyone knows. Just listen to the folks outside!

Townspeople's voices heard beyond wall.

Waitress
I heard Victor Hoffman was rejected
by the oldest Peterson girl.

Veteran
He worked for Jim Peterson and got fired.

Bus Driver
He made a deal with a lunatic.
Whoever got out first would wipe out
the Peterson family.

Sunday School Teacher
Victor didn't do it. He's a good boy.

Chorus
Victor's a bad boy.
Bad boy, bad boy, bad.

Veteran
Too bad Parliament just got rid
of the death penalty.

Young Victor
The mob could lynch me.

Older Victor
Brush the snow from your shoulders.
Remove your toque, your rubbers.
Come inside this hallowed house of justice.
Witness the trial of Victor Hoffman.

Scene 2
His Lordship

Wall opens. Spotlight on Judge.

Older Victor
Ah, there he is, Justice Murdoch Alexander McPherson Jr.
known to his friends as Sandy.

Young Victor
Lock him up.
See how he likes it.

Older Victor
Idiot! Listen! To what he didn't say at the trial.

His Lordship
Diefenbaker appointed me
when I was only forty-four. I didn't want
the court of appeal and to read law.
I prefer to sweat over live bodies.

Chorus
Bodies, bodies, bodies.

His Lordship
Take the accused before me.
No doubt he did it.

Older Victor
You killed nine people!

Young Victor
Pigs!

Sounds of pigs snuffling from Chorus.

His Lordship
Hoffman is likely legally insane,
but this panel of jurors might want revenge,
rather than the letter of the law.
The accused knew he was killing
but I doubt he knew he was killing people.

What could be worse than a mass murder trial
in northern Saskatchewan in January?
Cold hotels. Overcooked steak.
No Dorothy to soothe the savage
with mulled wine, the finest malt.
She tends to my body and soul as carefully
as she does her roses.

Young Victor
I never had a girlfriend, much less a wife.

His Lordship
I wish I were back in France with Dorothy
taking black and white photos of villages and peasants.
Though the farm wife might make a good shot,
poor soul. Everyone in my jurisdiction
a victim of a sullied system, a mental health sewer.
Even Dorothy might have been attacked
if the killer had gone to Regina
after his release from the asylum.

Young Victor
We're not going back there!

Older Victor
You'll go where I take you.

His Lordship
During the German occupation she vowed
to kiss the first allied soldier
who liberated the town of Le Touquet.

And there I was, Captain Sandy McPherson
of the second Canadian Corps.
It was three days after D-Day, September 5th.
She threw her arms around me and smooched me.

Young Victor
Close the wall! Shut him up!

Older Victor
Be patient.

Young Victor
You sound like Mum.

Older Victor
Why are you so mad?

Young Victor
He let me down. I wanted him
to be a hanging judge.

His Lordship
Dorothy would never wear
black patent boots, blue stockings,
like that Polish woman testifying.

Young Victor
There she is! There's my Mum.

His Lordship
Twenty-two years ago. Can it be that long?
My father and I defended the last man
hung here: Bootlegger Jack Loran.
He was convicted of capital murder
for killing a farmer during a robbery.
Like Hoffman, Loran heard voices,
but the court had no truck with psychiatry then.
Maybe I have a precedent-setting case now,

one that will help me forget
how I failed Jack Loran.

Young Victor
He failed me too.

> **Older Victor**
> Will anyone ever forget
> Victor Ernest Hoffman?

His Lordship
I've still got my World War II army rifle.
Waiting for some crazy bastard to come after you,
you'd damn well better be ready.

> **Older Victor**
> Are you ready?

Young Victor
This time, you can't make me do it.

> **Chorus**
> God does not love you, you you.

> **Older Victor**
> Why do you cling to them?

Young Victor
Why won't you let me go?

> **Older Victor**
> I got a day pass to the village.
> And I saw you, lurking on the street corner.
> You should never be let out like that.
> You, kid, are my demon.

Scene 3
The Prosecutor

Young Victor
You're as bad as the Crown prosecutor.
In black robes, he's just one more
of many persecutors.

He looks like the monk
who once jumped out of the ground.

> **Chorus**
> **One male voice:** It is I, Abel,
> shepherd of goats and sheep.
> You, tiller of soil.
> God does not love you.

>> **Older Victor**
> > The prosecutor had all the facts right!

Young Victor
When he visited me in jail
he wore a black coat like a magician's mantle,
collar turned up, prophet-eyes blazing.

> > **Older Victor**
> > He grew up on a farm near St. Walberg.
> > He played hockey and ball. So tough
> > he was the only player
> > other teams were scared of.

> > In summer, he strides around town bare-chested
> > flexing powerful biceps, so strong
> > he's not a man you'd want to tangle with in a bar.
> > When he orders five beer he holds up the hand
> > missing three fingers.

Young Victor
He could get me hanged!

Older Victor
He told me about another farm boy,
his mother dead, grieving father drunk,
beat him nightly, locked him
in the unheated attic,
with a mattress, a cup and plate.
The boy gave his dad fair warning:

Chorus
One voice: Stop. Or I'll shoot.

Sound of gunshot.

Older Victor
No charges laid. The prosecutor
found an aunt and uncle to take him in.
He earned his reputation
for being just.

Young Victor
He isn't fair to me.
He doped me up
so I can stand trial.

I can't turn my head
away from the prosecutor
without moving my body.

I need my mother's tea
towel around my head,
the knot between my teeth
to ease the pain of the swelling
in the right side of my brain.

Why won't anyone let me be
in peace?

I want my lawyer.

Scene 4
A Man Named Noble

Young Victor is in prisoner's box.

Older Victor
What can be said about a man
who suits his name?

Chorus
Angels: Noble, Noble, Noble.

Young Victor
He could be wearing a helmet.
He wields a sword
against my foes, accusers.

Older Victor
They say you can never go back,
never undo the past. Not true.
What happened goes wherever you go,
coming at you
when you least expect it,
whether you like it or not.

Young Victor
Whether you like it or not
Mr. Noble is on my side.

Older Victor

He interprets the Criminal Code
for twelve angry jurors
who can't understand
why no motive, no reason
for what you did to people you didn't know.

Young Victor

He's going to try to prove
I'm crazy. Will that set me free?

Older Victor

I don't want you released—ever!
Not unless—

Young Victor

—I find the right question?

Older Victor

That would be good for starters.

Scene 5
Exhibits

Young Victor remains in prisoner's box.

Older Victor

The Mounties wear blood-red serge to court.
Serge the name too of the prosecutor
wearing black silks, starched court tabs, ruffled cuffs.

Young Victor

I can't get my shirt collar to lie flat.
Grease stain on the pocket.
Shirt won't stay tucked in. My jeans

too tight in the waist.
My lawyer tried to make me
wear a suit to court.
So I'd look presentable.
I only wear my Sunday suit to church
to please my mother.

Older Victor
Listen to the witness!

Spotlight on Corporal McKenzie.

Corporal Roderick McKenzie
A twelve-year member of the RCMP
stationed at North Battleford,
in charge of the Identification Section
I take photographs, make charts
at scenes of crimes or suspected crimes.

On the 15th of August I proceeded
to the home of the Peterson family.

Young Victor
There in the yard an old combine, an outhouse.
On the front porch a washing machine.

Corporal McKenzie
My concern when taking the photograph
was to show the position of the corpse,
the footprint on the linoleum, its relationship
to the body, just beside the left hip of the deceased.
An imprint of a rubber boot in the blood on the floor.

Older Victor
Your bloody boots!

Young Victor
I can't turn my head

to look at the photo shown the court.
I'm scared the Haldol will curl back
my upper lip, bare my teeth
again. In a coyote snarl.

Older Victor
I don't have to look at photos
to remember rose-papered walls,
pictures of Mick Jagger, The Monkees,
Elizabeth Taylor, Bonanza stars.
Raggedy-Ann doll in a corner.
The baby's rocking horse.

Corporal McKenzie
These are the other items I found in the house:
A lead slug on the kitchen floor.
A spent .22-calibre casing under the father.
A cartridge casing under the chesterfield.
Two more casings under Jean's bed.
A slug under the mother and father's bed.

Beside the outside barrel in the corner
a slug on the ground under the baby, Larry,
two spent casings in the grass.

Here is the .22-caliber rifle taken
from the back seat of Victor Hoffman's
1950 grey Plymouth.
It's a Browning .22 pump action,
with CWN initialed on the stock,
serial number 26675 in front of the trigger.
I found seven live ones in the gun.

Young Victor
Numbers are as important as words.
My school at Kilwinning
was number 1392.
I failed Grades three and nine. Twice.

Older Victor
Don't play dumb!
You knew enough
to find the casings, throw them away,
hide the other evidence.

Corporal McKenzie
These are the rest of the exhibits:
A plastic bag containing seven vials
of bullets taken from the seven bodies.
A glass jar containing casings
the accused said he threw away.

Chorus
Away, away, away.

Older Victor
A dogmaster and police dog named Satan
searched north of the garage
for expended casings.

Young Victor
I led the cops to the wallets
I took from the bureau
and hid under a rock.

I tried to tell the Mounties
about the devil, how I saw him
looming above the blueberry bush,
and laughing he picked them all,
ate every one in my pail.

Hysterical laughter from Chorus.

I want to go home
to get a jar of my mum's preserves.

Older Victor

> **Older Victor**
> Bawl-baby! I'm sick of you.

Spotlight on McKenzie goes to black, then lights up on George Edward Noble.

> **Older Victor**
> At least Defence Counsel has no objections
> to the Crown's exhibits.

George Edward Noble
Why didn't anyone tell Victor he was under arrest?
Why wasn't a lawyer present
when they taped his confession? If they knew the accused
had been incarcerated
in Saskatchewan Hospital
why didn't they call a doctor?

Young Victor
Those were the wrong questions?

George Edward Noble
Even if Victor didn't show any feelings,
didn't break down under questioning,
didn't he talk about satan,
supernatural powers?
No threats, no harsh words?
If they led Victor to believe
they had evidence
—the boots, the rifle—
wasn't that an inducement to confess?

Young Victor
They scared me!

It doesn't matter
how hard it blows outside,

the window casings
hold tight, radiators
steam full blast,
hissing:

> **Chorus**
> Satan, satan, satan.
> Only satan. Only his say
> must be obeyed.

> > **Older Victor** *Visibly afraid.*
> > Snap out of it!
> > Come to your senses!

Scene 6
Ballistics

Young Victor
I've had enough!

> > **Older Victor**
> > The trial is never over.

Young Victor
It could be if you ever stop punishing me.
You always blame me. Just like Dad.

> > **Older Victor**
> > He and Mum were scared
> > when you took off on them.

Young Victor
After I got home
Mum scolded me
for getting up so early,

for driving. Dad gave me heck
for carrying a loaded gun in the car.

I never do anything right.

I knew I'd hurt my family.
I milked the cows, it was hard
because of the murders. I cried.
Couldn't eat breakfast.
I paced. Scared. I felt rotten.

Older Victor
You're a murderer.

Young Victor
The police would fire the gun,
would do ballistic tests.

Older Victor
The ballistics expert was Sergeant Shayne Kirby.

Spotlight on Sergeant Kirby.

Sergeant Shayne Kirby
I'm in charge of the firearms section
of the Crime Detection Laboratory.
The rifle is a Browning model 2200,
introduced in Canada about 1922.
It's a .22 pump action,
with CWN initialed on the stock,
serial number 26675 in front of the trigger.

Young Victor
Bang bang bang
it just went bang
in my head.

Sound of gunshots.

Chorus
Kill, kill, kill.

Sergeant Kirby
In function-firing, I got no misfires,
no hangfires, no failures to eject.
It had some work done on it
by an amateur
in mounting bases for a scope.

Young Victor
Amateur! I don't think so.
I made my first gun from two old ones,
same as I made a bicycle-built-for-two
with two old bikes. A motorcycle
by attaching a washing machine
motor to a bicycle.

Sergeant Kirby
All imperfections. Scratch marks,
tool marks, rust, corrosion,
give a signature
for a particular barrel.

Older Victor
That gun had my name on it.

Young Victor
My mind runs away a lot.
I remember things happening before they happen.
I knew they would come and get me.

They locked me up.
The cops talked to me nice.
Like I was a real human being.

In jail the cops had two Sam Brown holsters
hanging on an oak costumer, they called it.

I could have taken one. Killed them all.

Chorus
Kill, kill, kill.

Sergeant Kirby
The bullets taken from the bodies
were fired from the rifle.

Young Victor
My dad only hit me once.
I can talk to my mother.
She's like me. Doesn't talk
well to other people.

                                    Older Victor
                          I don't want you to ever see
                                the outside world again.

Young Victor
I should have been hanged.

                                    Older Victor
                                   For what? Say it!

Young Victor
I killed—cats.

Scene 7
Chemistry

Young Victor
A cat is an animal
that can really fall
in love with you.

When I play rough
they lose their love for me.
A dog will attack or try to bite you,
but a cat will stare, yellow-green eyes
in the dark like glass. Cats you can hypnotize
with a mirror. Send them flying! Bouncing
off the ceiling! Hitting the walls!

Chorus makes sounds of dying cats.

For days I locked a cat
in the garage. Starved it.
I wanted to die too.

I had a chemistry set once.
Experimented on cats
before I took it myself. The stuff
really made cats crazy.
Eyes rolled in their heads.
They didn't die.
I had to club them. Kick them.
Stomp on them with my rubber boots.

Older Victor
Look at the wall!

Spotlight on Beverly Long.

Beverly Jean Long
I'm employed at the Crime Detection Laboratory
in the Serology Department.
Exhibit P15 is a pair of rubber boots.
I tested for the presence of blood.

Young Victor
My dad wanted me to be a man,
but I didn't like hunting, killing deer.
I'd shoot at anything else: hawks, rocks, cans.

I never shot a coyote.
Squirrels were something else again,
like rats they carry disease.
I had to keep the numbers down.
Dad wanted me to get rid of the cats,
too many of them with frozen ears,
messing in Mum's laundry basket.

Dad bawled me out for shooting too much
so I started stealing ammunition
from Mansell's hardware store in Leask.

Older Victor
You never learn.

Beverly Jean Long
Exhibit P26 is a gas pedal
from the 1950 Plymouth
seized in the Hoffman yard.

Examining it for the presence of blood
I obtained a positive result
in the area marked with a red grease pencil.

Older Victor
More proof, kid.

Young Victor
I had a shiny stone once.
The devil never wanted me
to have anything, not even a toboggan.
He took it, the shiny stone.
I threw a net over the devil
and took away his magic.
His guardian devil threw me down
Judo-like. Picked me right up
off the ground. The devil got away.
But he always returns.

Yeah, wearin' my boots.

Spotlight on Corporal Mooney.

Corporal George Robert Mooney
I'm from the Hair and Fibre Section
of the Crime Detection Laboratory.
I produced bootprints
by inking battleship linoleum
then had a person
walk these boots on the ink
then onto pieces of paper.

Young Victor
Oh good, the janitor story.

Spotlight on RCMP Janitor.

RCMP Janitor
Now, I'm a practical sort of guy.
Never dream at night. Sleep.
Like a baby. Nothin' gets to me,
not even blood. I just clean up
after them experts. I was some freaked
when this scientific cop asks me to put on rubber boots
that belonged to the Shell Lake Murderer.

They say youse can't know a feller
till you've walked a mile in his shoes.
Well sir, I shook so bad
I could hardly get my runners offa
my feet. He let me keep my socks on.
So I says to the scientist, I says,
"them boots won't fit." An' he says,
"Just give 'em a try."

Be damned if them boots don't fit like a glove.
My knees knockin' so bad

I can hardly stand up.
He lifts one foot, then t'other.
Maybe they'll make me do somethin' awful.
Turn me into a killer. I'm so mad
I could just shoot somebody. Till it's done
and it's my footprints on the paper.

Older Victor
Your bootprints, kid.

Young Victor
It's like my whole body was cut in half.
Something had left me. Powerful.
The impulse to kill.

Chorus
Kill, kill, kill.

Older Victor
I don't think you heard
one word of the evidence
against you.

Young Victor
Who do you think you are? The prosecutor?

Don't you know there's a war
going on? Between the devils and angels!

Older Victor
Where are they now?

Young Victor
Oh, they're everywhere!
The devils go back to hell
and sometimes They come back.
They rule!

Laughter from the Chorus.

Older Victor

It's time you listened to dad.
He always said there are no devils,
except maybe you.

Scene 8
You Could Understand Him, But It Made No Sense

Wall opens, spotlight on Robert Hoffman.
On the witness stand he wears his Sunday suit, bow tie askew, work-
worn hands clasped
as if in prayer.

Older Victor

Dad looks like I do now, same long nose,
same sheep-shear haircut,
forehead soft as a sow's udder.
He looks broken. Ragged. Jowls slack,
mouth sagging at the corners.
He likely hasn't slept much since last August.

Pause.

Look at him!

Young Victor
I don't even know my father. My mum
told me he was born in Russia in 1911.
That's some long time ago, some far away
where them spies live. Dad, he comes
to Canada with Grandma Emma and Grandpa
Reinhold. They settled in Silvergrove.
Eldest of ten children, Dad had to quit school,
just like me, to work on the farm. But he

don't even know me. We aren't alike at all.

Robert Hoffman
My son Victor is the fourth of seven children:
Eileen, Richard and Marion, Lorraine,
then come Victor Ernest, Bernice, and finally Allen.
As a baby, Victor threw tantrums,
banged his head on floor. Pulled out his hair.

Young Victor
I know all that stuff.

Older Victor
Wait!

Robert Hoffman
He grew up fast, like a blade of grass.
Mr. Noble, you said I should describe him
to the court as a shy sort of boy.
No friends. Didn't date, drink, smoke.
He liked to be alone, that's all I figure.

Young Victor
I'm a loner,
don't run with the pack,
they'll turn on you
if you don't watch it.

Robert Hoffman
Whenever I asked him to do something,
he'd be right there. He would never say no
and would do a good job.

Older Victor
See! He's proud of you.

Young Victor
Why didn't he tell me that before?

Hell, nothin' pleased him.

Robert Hoffman
Once, he picked forty acres of roots.
Back-breakin' work.

He used to talk to himself.
I saw him in the one-ton truck, laughin'.
I asked him to tell me the joke,
but he slammed the truck into gear.
He just about run over his brother.

Young Victor
I sent that sucker flyin' outta my way,
a devil-bat from Hell.

Hissing from the Chorus.

> **Older Victor**
> It was your brother!

Young Victor
Was not!

Robert Hoffman
Restless, he'd drive off in the car
without tellin' anyone where he was going.
Or where he'd been when he got back.

Young Victor
As if anyone would believe me.

Robert Hoffman
Victor never did talk much.
He'd answer your questions,
but that's about all.
You could understand him,

but it made no sense.

When Robert Hoffman leaves the witness stand he passes close to Young Victor in the prisoner's box.

Young Victor
Dad! Just find one of the diamonds.
That's all you have to do. Look in the bush by the barrel.
That will explain everything.
You'll know the devil is real!

                                    Old Victor
                    What did the shrinks say about that? The devil
                                              was real?

Young Victor
Sure as hell!

Scene 9
In Her Own House

Wall open, spotlight on Stella Hoffman.

Stella Hoffman
How can I ever
lift my head again,
speak before all these people?
If it will help Victor
I'll tell the court how sick my son.

Young Victor
Once, I was throwing darts.
She almost walked
right into one. Did she ever
give me a scare.

Stella Hoffman
When he fell
from a cottonwood tree
and cut his hip, he told no one
he was hurt. I saw him limping
and asked him to take down his trousers.
I'd cut them off with a scissors,
if he wouldn't obey me. I told him
he could die from blood poisoning.

Young Victor
You wouldn't have cared.

> **Older Victor**
> She always cared!

Young Victor
Another time she went to get the cows.
I was shooting magpies.
A bullet ricocheted off the granary.
Just missed her.

Stella Hoffman
Until the killings,
giving birth to Victor
was the worst thing
that ever happened to me.
Not like the other children
he didn't fight for
his first breath.

Young Victor
I'd have to be crazy
to want to live
with demon-pigs. I don't mind
the angels.

Stella Hoffman
I worried more about Victor
than all the other children
put together.

Young Victor
I got super strength.
I threw a crowbar
like a javelin.
I screamed, "Mother!"

> **Older Victor**
> Stop!

Stella Hoffman
I could never reason with him.
He wouldn't listen when I told him:
stealing ammunition is wrong.

Young Victor
Dad says I shoot too much.
He won't let me buy bullets.
How else do I prove
I'm a man?

Stella Hoffman
I'd bawl him out
for coming home late:
Don't you know
how worried I was?

Young Victor
I get so scared
when devils attack angels
I gotta get away.

> **Older Victor**
> Face them. Get rid of them.

Young Victor
I tried. The bullets went right though them.

Older Victor
That's not how to do it.

Stella Hoffman
Why couldn't he try
to please his dad?
Instead of doing everything
to make him angry, lying—

Young Victor
The angel's blouse was torn
when I tried to save her.

Stella Hoffman
When he came home from hospital
he was not right;
he was still sick.
They said Victor had to take his pills,
but never told us
how important it was—

Older Victor
—to keep me away from guns.

Stella Hoffman
It would have been only
a matter of seconds for them.

Older Victor
You never would have killed
those innocent people.

Stella Hoffman
He even wanted to killed us.

The Saturday—before it happened—
was seeding time. Victor was working
with chemicals. He got terrible sick.

Young Victor
Nothing worked. Not them shocks.
Never the pills.

Stella Hoffman
When the news of the murders broke
Robert put a latch on the porch door
always left open before. All that time
the killer was in our own house.

Why wasn't he helped as he should have been?

Young Victor
Mum asked the question!

> **Older Victor**
> No one heard her.
> No one answered.

Young Victor
You lied to me! Said
all I had to do was find
the right question.

> **Older Victor**
> Here's Hoffer,

Scene 10
Working For A Higher Injunction

Wall opens, spotlight on Dr. Abraham Hoffer.

Older Victor
Dr. Abraham Hoffer doesn't look like a hippie,
the man who coined the word: psychedelic.
The morning news likely didn't help his mood:
DEMANDS BY PROVINCES FOR EXTRA MEDICARE
FUNDS REJECTED BY OTTAWA.
No mention of mental health,
there never is, just listen to the shrinks
gobbling like geese when you catch them.

Dr. Hoffer
Victor Hoffman was acting mechanically.
I don't think he was capable of feeling any emotion.
A robot programmed to kill and not get caught
could have done exactly what he did.

Young Victor
I was scared!

Dr. Hoffer
The murders were a series of random events.
I don't think they were planned in any way.

He told me he did not feel guilty. Robbery
was evil and against the law, killing was not.

He was doing what he had to do in terms
of the delusions he suffered. His victims
did not look like people. They looked rotten
he said, pig-like.

Sound of pigs snorting from Chorus.

Young Victor *Imitating Older Victor.*
Listen to the witness.

Dr. Hoffer
I'm convinced he saw the devil.
He was real to him. He heard voices.

Chorus
We're still here, here, here.

                                      Older Victor
In Dr. Hoffer's office, I turned to stone,
like the marker over the common grave
of the nine Petersons.

Young Victor
He made me so mad when he said:
"The devil doesn't exist."
I saw satan! He was real!

Dr. Hoffer
I do not think Victor Hoffman clearly separated in his mind
the acts of killing birds, dogs, cows, or people.
I don't think he really thought he was killing a human.
The cries and pleading for mercy elicited no emotion
in him. Seeing what he had done, or possibly the victims'
slow deaths, snapped him back to reality. Even then
he felt no emotion, only acted mechanically
to escape detection.

He appreciated the nature of the act, not its quality.
He was working for a higher injunction
which set him apart from the ordinary man.

                                       Older Victor
There was a moment, just one
after which nothing was the same again.
No one heard the warning.

Young Victor
Mum and Dad saw me shooting the devil-pigs!

      Chorus
When, when, when, when.
Seek and ye shall find find find
The when, when, when.

Older Victor

You only really listen to the doctors.
You make me so mad I could just—

Young Victor *Laughing.*
—shoot me!

Older Victor

"The time has come," the walrus said.

Young Victor
Wait! There's Dr. McKerracher.

Scene 11
The Man from Mount Blackstrap

Wall opens, spotlight on Dr. McKerracher.
Awkward and gangly, the paper-thin professor
stumbles to the witness stand.

Older Victor

Professor Donald Griffith McKerracher is a god
in the annals of mental health history.
Just ask some of his successors,
patients, students, families who still dream
of something better than the street,
the institution without walls.

They have never heard of his Saskatchewan Plan.
The bag lady fishing in a garbage can.
The ragged man sleeping under a bridge.
The boy in an unfinished basement
lying on a cot next to a deer carcass
hung to age by the operator
of an unapproved boarding house.
The people in soup kitchens.

He looks like Lincoln, chiselled in marble,
his credentials as long as a myth with no end.

Young Victor
Dr. McKerracher can see right through you.

Older Victor
An accident of birth.
He has damaged optic muscles.

Young Victor
It's hard to tell who he's looking at:
the judge or jury, Mr. Noble, or me.
Maybe he's trying to look over his shoulders
to see who is following him.
His eyes shoot in different directions.

Dr. McKerracher seems to care
even more than Mr. Noble
about whether I go to prison
or back to the nut house.

Dr. McKerracher
The hospital at North Battleford failed
at treatment even before Hoffman, admission
too difficult, the practice of early discharge
with no follow-up an indictment
of a medical disaster. Witness: Shell Lake.

He had to kill and kill and kill.
He thought he was acting
as an agent of the devil.

The thought of wrongness
just would not have crossed his mind.

Older Victor
Yet, in McKerracher's office
I howled for half a day.

Young Victor
Bring in Noble!

Scene 12
May It Please The Jury

Young Victor
Holy Cow! The courthouse is packed
to the rafters, with people
leaning against walls,
kneeling on the fringe
of the public gallery,
crammed in the doorway. The hall.
A hush. Mr. Noble begins his defence.

Spotlight on George Edward Noble.

Mr. Noble
Thank you for your due care
in a grave and serious trial.

Young Victor
Don't mention it.

> **Older Victor**
> He's thanking the jury, Dope!

Young Victor
As if I could escape
these handcuffs.
Mounties wear bullet-
proof vests, their brawny
bodies between me
and the public gallery.
My parents received
so many threats
the cops are afraid.

Mr. Noble
This case has achieved notoriety.
Publicity swirls about you
while you concentrate on the evidence.

Young Victor
The Press scratch on paper, so many
chickens scrabbling in dirt for kernels.
Daily, they crucify me
for showing no feeling.

Young Victor rattles his handcuffs.

I can only shift one foot
stretching muscles stiff from Haldol.
I'm afraid. Again. Of falling
into the blue.

My upper lip might turn up
in a fang-bared snarl. Spit leaking.
My mouth is so dry.

Mr. Noble
The accused stands charged
on two counts of non-capital murder.
I do not quarrel with the Crown's evidence
nor with the claim that James and Evelyn Peterson
died early that morning of August 15th
as a result of gunshot wounds
fired from a gun
in the hands of Victor Hoffman.

Older Victor
The prosecutor has feathery eyebrows,
hooded lids. Like my raptor
watching it all
from the Peterson's yard pole.

Young Victor
It could alight on the railing.
I could get it in my sights.
Shoot it.

     Chorus
     No, no, no, it's too small, small, small.

Young Victor
The jury's staring at me!

                    Older Victor
               As if I'm the two-headed dog
               created by Soviet scientists
            who attached head and front legs
               of a two-month-old puppy
                onto a four-year-old dog.
                The puppy bit the dog's ear.

Mr. Noble
The Criminal Code says: "No person
shall be convicted of an offence
while he is insane. Everyone shall,
until the contrary is proved,
be presumed to be sane."

                    Older Victor
                  At home now
              cows chew their cud,
           waiting for fresh well water
             pumped into their trough.
          For the first lap of the tongue
       on a saltlick. Cows aren't as stupid
         as you think. Yet, easy to herd.

Young Victor
Herd. The last name
of the guy, Clarence,

who tore his blanket,
hung himself from
the horizontal bar
at the front of his cell.

Cops found the body
this morning.

Mr. Noble
A person is insane in law
when he has a disease of the mind
that renders him incapable of appreciating
the nature and quality of an act
or of knowing that an act was wrong.

Why? We must ask, does a shy, unsophisticated
farm boy suddenly and senselessly
take the lives of people he doesn't know
and has never even heard of?

Young Victor
Herd was crazy
to hang himself.
Serving a two-year sentence
for possession of stolen goods
he was due for release in June.

Blanket. Belt. Rope. Hope
for a better way to die.

Muted sounds of animals dying from Chorus.

Mr. Noble
Why? We must ask, does this boy,
this hard-working, obedient boy,
who is in no sense a criminal
do such a thing?

Young Victor
It popped into my mind
just like that. Do you think I could get rid of it?

Older Victor
Why why why why.
Cat in the barn. Crouched
before a moth, ready to spring,
whiskers twitching, powerful back legs
tensed. It leaps suddenly
to a height undreamed
by the insect caught.

Mr. Noble peers at Victor over his black cat-eye glasses.

Mr. Noble
Why? We must ask, did events
on that fateful morning
lead him to Shell Lake
where he had never been before
and into the home of the Petersons
so far from the area in which he lived
and played and worked his whole life?
Why? What compelled this man?

Young Victor
I was looking for spruce trees
and just bang like that,
my mind went on to kill.

Gunshots.

*Mr. Noble pauses at prisoner's box,
his arm and hand on its railing.*

Young Victor
Look! Mr. Noble wears a wedding band.

Older Victor
His soft hands never milked a cow,
pounded a fence post, bent a horseshoe.

Mr. Noble
He was diagnosed as a chronic schizophrenic,
a disease of the mind, of long duration.

I suggest to you that no one who has heard the evidence
can possibly doubt that to him his hallucinations were real
and terrifying. You will recall how he described the devil.
Over six feet. Big. Black. Naked. The devil.

Chorus
Devil-Pigs: You belong to us, us, us.

Young Victor
First time I saw the devil
I was ten, eating breakfast.
So scared. I ran outside.

I planned to catch satan
when I got out of the hospital.
With a net, a bear trap, poison.

Mr. Noble
Victor was trying to tell the truth
as he understood it.

Young Victor
Only Mum ever understood my fear.
What would happen if Dad died?
I would run the farm,
and I couldn't do anything right.

"Mum, don't make me
cut the heads of chickens!"

Chorus makes sounds of dying chickens.

Older Victor

After the axe. The head on the block
still squawks. Body crazy-
wild. Flapping. Wings.
Feathers flying and falling.
It flops dead as a stone.

Mr. Noble
It may seem peculiar
that Victor can remember what happened
when he was in an acute state of reaction.
The memory is not impaired
even as he moves from reality
into unreality and back again.

Young Victor
Stealing is wrong. You go to jail.
Killing devils to save the angels
might get you into heaven. Might not.

Older Victor

That's enough!
You know the difference between being sick and well
so why can't you tell the difference between being guilty
and making excuses and taking responsibility?

Young Victor
You think you're so smart.
Listen to Mr. Noble.

Mr. Noble
He acted without anger, without elation.

Young Victor
I was scared, not sorry.
The devil-pig had me by the throat.

Mr. Noble
He began to come to his senses

when he was shaking out the blankets
and saw Phyllis.

Young Victor
She was only a little girl.
I'd never hurt a child.

Older Victor
You killed seven children!

Young Victor
My confession was four days later.
They locked me up.
Took fingerprints.
Ink smeared like blood
across the sky.

Mr. Noble
Who would kill for seven dollars?
Victor had money.
He did not turn the house upside down
looking for valuables.

Gentlemen, our law is a humane law.

Young Victor
I bawled over sick calves
shot in the head.

Mr. Noble
The defense of insanity is not raised
as a last resort. We do not deny the tragedy.
If you ask yourself why
on the burden of evidence
you are left with only one conclusion:
the accused was insane,
legally insane when he did it.

> **Older Victor**
> I don't get it.
>
> Why is there a difference between legal insanity
> and being morally insane?
> I look at you every day of my life here,
> and you remind me that I'm a killer.
> I did it! And if you cheek your pills
> then spit them into the toilet,
> you could do it again.

Mr. Noble
May it now please the court.

> **Older Victor**
> No! May it now please me!
> Call Wildrew Lange.

Scene 13
The Testimony of Wildrew Lange

Young Victor
Every day, my trial plays over and over again.
Like a Hi-Fi with a wobbly turntable,
a scratched seventy-eight record,
the needle jumping,
from band to band.

> **Chorus**
> **Devil-pig:** You can't get rid of me, me, me.
> **Angel:** I'm still here, here, here.
> **Devil-pig:** Run, run as fast as you can. You're not
> even a man, man, man.

Young Victor
Barely aware of my case

before the court,
I only feel as if I'm drifting
like snow swept by angel wings
across the Peterson graves.

Spotlight on Wildrew Lange.

Wildrew Lange
My name is Wildrew, not Wilfred.
I'm thirty-five. Yes, I'm a farmer
at Shell Lake. Lived there all my life,
not too far from the Petersons.
Oh, I'd say a little over three miles.
I think Jim come here
after the army, that would be '46.
So I knew him for about eighteen years.
Yes, I knew his wife Evelyn and kids:
Dorothy, Mary, William, Colin,
Larry, Phyllis, Jean, and Pearl.
Yes, seven children.

> **Older Victor.**
> People! Children!

Young Victor
When I went into that house
I didn't see people.

Wildrew Lange
I made arrangements to meet Jim
at a granary, not a hayfield.
No! Not a hayfield, a grain bin.

Jim wasn't there as I expected,
so I cleaned out one bin,
then drove to the Peterson yard.
I went up to the porch door, knocked,
and there was no answer.

I knocked again, opened the door.
I saw Jim—laying on the floor—dead.
Just had his shorts on.
Lying on his stomach. Yes, he was dead.
Quite a lot of blood.

Chorus
Blood, blood, blood.

Young Victor
I left the devil-pig lying face down,
forehead pressed against the leg of a chair,
left hand under his chin,
right arm reaching for a sealer top,
hand closing on a dirty rag.

Older Victor
When it was done, the giant pigs gone,
you saw the real man.
Skin marble white
except for face, neck
wind-burned. Forearms
red to the elbows.
He always rolled his sleeves up, a sign
of a hard worker.
Dark hair cropped.

Young Victor
I'm letting mine grow long.
I hate the way my dad cut it.
He might as well have used sheep shears.
Looks so bad I couldn't smile
in the last family photo.

Older Victor
The man! The man!
His name was Jim.

Young Victor
Jim? Are you sure?

Wildrew Lange
I took Jim's car and went into town,
phoned the Mountie in Spiritwood.
I stopped Corporal Richards on the highway,
and told him what I seen. He went into the house.
Yes, then he came out.
He said they were all—dead.

> **Chorus**
> Dead, dead, dead.

He went to town to phone up to Battleford
for help and a doctor.
Then he went back in a second time,
brought out four-year-old Phyllis.

Young Victor
I spared her.

> **Older Victor**
> She was a real person?
> Not a hawk, a squirrel, a coyote.
> Never a pig?

Young Victor
Of course.

> **Older Victor**
> And the others?

Young Victor
Demons. Piglets. With horns!
I'm sure of it.

> **Older Victor**
> Next Witness!

Scene 14
Pathology

Spotlight on Dr. Oliver Lane.

Dr. Oliver Lane
My name is Dr. Oliver Guy Lane.
I'm a pathologist in Prince Albert.
Starting with James Peterson:
a man of forty-seven years of age,
height five feet ten and a half inches,
weight 170 pounds.
I found eleven gunshot wounds
in the head, neck, chest,
arm, left leg, derma.

Young Victor
It was a big black devil-pig.
Naked on the bed. Not a real man.
It said:

> **Chorus**
> **One voice:** Who is it?

Young Victor
It jumped up when it saw my gun.

> **Chorus**
> **One voice:** Don't shoot me!

Young Victor
It kept coming at me.
It grabbed me by the neck here.
I kept on shooting at it.
Until the gun was empty.

Sound of gunshots.

It's quicker if you shoot to the head
of an animal, or in its heart.
That way it won't suffer.

Chorus
One male voice: I don't want to die.

Older Victor
A pig can't talk.

Young Victor
What kind of a doctor
prefers to cut up the dead?
After they hang me
will my body lie
on a metal examining table?
Rope burns around the neck.
Eyes bulging out of their sockets.
The cause of death: asphyxiation.
Spinal cord snapped?

Chorus
Dead, dead, dead as dead.

Dr. Lane
Evelyn Peterson, the mother, was a normal-
appearing, middle-aged female, slightly obese.
She had five gunshot wounds
on the face, in the right ear,
at the junction of the nose and face,
in the lower part of the back.
One just to the right of the jaw,
another between the corner
of the mouth and the point of the chin.

Young Victor
She was the fat one

who tried to escape
out the window. With a bundle
I didn't know was a human baby.
The shot to the back
didn't stop her
from begging me
not to kill her.

> **Chorus**
> **One female voice:** Please. No! Please don't!

> > **Older Victor**
> > She saw you? She could identify you?

Sound of baby crying from Chorus.

Young Victor
I had to finish it off, the baby,
because nobody might find it
for three or four days. It would starve.
I wish I had taken it in the car,
left it beside the road
for someone to find.

> > **Older Victor**
> > Then what did you do?

Muted sounds of piglets squealing from Chorus.

Young Victor
I went on killing,
unable to stop,
until I was spent.

Dr. Lane
I examined the seven children.
Each had gunshot wounds in the head.

> **Older Victor**
> Admit it! You killed seven children!

Chorus: Sounds of piglets slowly change to children's screams under gunshots.

Young Victor *Breaking down.*
Oh God, they tried to help
each other, the oldest girl using her body
like a shield. Grasping. They touched,
a boy died with his hand on another's ankle.
A middle-sized girl lay her head
on an older girl's belly.

> **Older Victor**
> Like a tumble of squirming puppies
> squalling after their tails were cut off.

Young Victor *On his knees.*
Make them stop!

Young Victor begins to make sounds of an animal in pain, a lowing, then rising to sound of coyote's long howl which rises over Chorus offstage:

> **Chorus** *Female Voices in unison*
> —Help! Daddy! Mummy! *BANG*
> —Don't shoot me! *BANG*
> —Stop! Don't! Please! *BANG*
> —Jean, help me! *BANG*
> —I can't. Daddy! Somebody! *BANG*
> —Make him go away. *BANG*

Then silence.

Young Victor
I saw the yellow coyote out the window, watching.

108   The Room With Five Walls

Older Victor

Then you saw all the blood.

Bodies.

Young Victor

The shock! They died—so hard.

I want a bullet to my head.

Older Victor

George Edward Noble won.

I was found not guilty by reason of insanity.

I didn't understand the pleasure

of the Lieutenant Governor.

The Attorney General washed his hands

of Victor Ernest Hoffman.

Chorus

One voice: Get rid of him!

Older Victor

Saskatchewan Hospital couldn't hold me.

I was shipped here

to the maximum security prison

for the criminally insane. The Ridge!

Where I have to help us

through this.

Young Victor

There are some things worse than death.

Older Victor

I have to live with you.

Scene 15
Phantom Fighting

Young Victor
I know what you want from me now.
I'm not into fighting phantoms.
So just knock it off.

Older Victor glares at Young Victor
who jerks his head sideways as if slapped.

Ow! Why'd you have to go and hit me?

                                          Older Victor
                              I want you to fight with your soul.

Young Victor
I'm outta here!

                                          Older Victor
                                          Not on your life.

Older Victor doesn't move or touch
Young Victor, but Young Victor takes
a blow to the jaw, an uppercut to his chin,
a punch in the belly. He falls.

Young Victor
How'd you do that?

                                          Older Victor
                                          Do it with your mind.

Older Victor turns binoculars on the wall. It turns blue. Behind the
smoke screen an illusion may be created of angels descending on sil-
ver ladders, ropes. The earth opens, red smoke create a similar illu-
sion of devil-pigs rising. Chorus voices speak in unison, softly at first,
then growing louder. Young Victor cowers.

Chorus
Angel: Victor, Victor, I've come for you, you, you.
Devil: God does not love you, you, you.
All: We do, do, do.
Devil: Kill, kill,kill.
Shoot something big, big, big, big.
Do it now, now, now, now.
Angel: I'm always here, here, here, here.

Young Victor
I want to go home!

Older Victor
Stand up! Face them!

Young Victor
I can't! They rule.
They must be obeyed.

Older Victor
Look at them!

Chorus hisses.

Young Victor
Then they'll have me.

Older Victor
Fight them!

Young Victor
Go away!

Chorus voices lower, they begin to back off.

Older Victor
What did you tell the cops?

Young Victor
I can never kill again.
Why can't anyone understand
I was spent. Emptied like the gun.
For God's sake, believe me.

Older Victor
Show me. Show them.

Young Victor faces Chorus.
He shadow boxes, swinging widly.
Laughter from the Chorus.

.

Older Victor
No. Hold perfectly still.
Do it with your mind.

When smoke clears, phantoms are gone. Empty silver ladders rise
and disappear. Red and blue lights slowly fade. Then black. Sound
of wall closing.

Young Victor
They're gone. I can't hear them.

Older Victor
They'll be back.
We'll fight them again
tomorrow and the next day.
For now, come with me.

Fall into the blue
of a winter day
where the sky is so deep
you can fall right into it.

Sound of rooster crowing.

Older Victor
At home, the cock crows at first light.
Time for chores.
Cows' udders full to bursting.
I press my forehead
against a Hereford's warm and soughing belly.
The squeeze of the soft teats, a balm to my hands
sore from pulling roots, chopping kindling
for Mum's stove.
I find comfort in the smell of hay,
the dark corner stall,
watched only by barn cats.

Young Victor
I can never go home.

Acknowledgements

I am indebted to Mr. Justice George Edward Noble, who was the defence counsel for Victor Hoffman. For many years, he kept in touch with his client and followed the progress of his recovery. His stories of the trial captured my imagination and empathy for the accused, and when he offered the complete file of public documents it was a gift I couldn't refuse; hence this poetic drama.

The justices of North Battleford remembered for me the history of the courthouse. Special thanks to Mr. Justice Dennis Maher, who was the prosecutor's assistant during the trial, and to Dr. David Keegan for his continuing support and reading of the original monologues and psychiatrists' testimonies.

While I have tried to adhere faithfully to the Shell Lake events and the facts of the trial, this is an attempt to explore the questions that might have been raised rather than expose or reveal the real man, then or now. The letters he wrote to his parents are adapted poetically from originals contained in his legal files, with permission of Justice Noble. I must also acknowledge Peter Tadman's True Crime edition, *The Shell Lake Massacre*, in which I learned about the cats and the rape in the boys' bathroom.

The life of the deceased Peterson family and the suffering of the surviving Petersons has, through the years, been sensationalised in newspapers, tabloids, magazines, and published books of non-fiction. Out of respect for their privacy, I have concentrated entirely on Victor's story as it might have been told.

I am truly grateful to the Poets' Combine, Judith Krause, Bruce Rice, Paul Wilson, Gary Hyland, and Robert Currie, who read and critiqued many poems, and to Sean Virgo for the suggestion to create a poetic drama. Thanks too, to Brenda Niskala for the Monday lunches, with poetry.

CBC producer Kelly Jo Burke led me to the redemptive spirit contained in the phantom fight.

I wish to acknowledge the Saskatchewan Playwrights

Centre, dramaturge Ben Henderson for his in-depth analysis and insights, the wonderful actors who assisted in the development of this play through workshops that led to the 2002 Spring Festival of New Plays, especially the inimitable Kelly Henderek and inspiring Michele Sereda. I wish to thank amazing Artistic Director Linda Moore who showed me the way to the dramatic pulse of the play.

Finally, to Michele Sereda, Curtain Razors and the University of Regina for producing the play in 2004, my publisher NeWest Press for another leap of faith, and editor Lynne Van Luven because we've come a long way since the days of English 584.

Byrna Barclay

BYRNA BARCLAY is the award-winning author of three novels and three short story collections. Her fiction and poetry have appeared in numerous literary magazines and anthologies. She has served as president of the Saskatchewan Writer's Guild and is currently a board member of the Saskatchewan Playwright's Centre. A strong advocate for mental health reform, she served as the President of the Canadian Mental Health Association in Saskatchewan, was the founding chair of the Mental Health Advisory Council, and is the Editor-in-chief of *Transition Magazine*. The mother of two grown children, she and her husband have made their home in Regina, Saskatchewan since 1962.

Other books by Byrna Barclay

Summer of the Hungry Pup, published by NeWest Press in 1982.

The Last Echo, published by NeWest Press in 1984.

Winter of the White Wolf, published by NeWest Press in 1986.

From the Belly of a Flying Whale, published by Douglas &
    McIntyre in 1985.

Crosswinds, published by Coteau Books in 1995

searching for the nude in the landscape, published by
    Thistledown Press in 1996.